Not a Humpty Dumpty

Anne-Lise Collins

The Archway

The Archway 2006

First edition

Contents

Introduction

My book has three parts. In the first part I describe my childhood and youth in Norway and my early married life in England. In the second part I talk about how my growing faith enabled me to overcome the great tragedies of my life. In the third part I pay homage to the people who have influenced me over the years.

I am so grateful to God for the way he has helped me through some difficult circumstances. It is my hope that this book will help other grieving relatives come to terms with the sadness of living through a family member leaving this life. God will give you that strength. He is able to give you much more than you can ever hope or imagine.

Like Humpty Dumpty, I fell off the wall and broke into a thousand pieces but God lovingly put the pieces together and put me back on the wall. When pottery is broken and glued together it is stronger than before it was broken. As a person you are also more able to cope with stressful circumstances when you have had to face the worst, it makes you more resilient.

At first I thought that if I felt sad it would only be self-pity but I had to learn that Christians also have to suffer grief. Until then my I had avoided thinking about it. Now I had to face the truth. It was like going down a slope where it was dark, going through the pain and heartbreak and slowly going up the slope the other end. Without the Lord's help and my children I would not have made it. There is a very helpful little book called Living through Grief. It takes you through the various stages of grief and makes you feel less lonely. It is reassuring to find out that you are not the only one who has had to cope with similar feelings.

I am not in the same league as the other people in this book. Some far outshine the rest of us. My reason for including them is that not many people would want to read about me, so I started looking around for people to write about who have been and are excellent examples of what I mean by being "Not Humpty Dumpty".

There are many you do not hear about who go through great tragedies, but with God's help, survive and triumph over the circumstances by giving their all to other people. I have included some I know and trust you will enjoy reading about them.

My reason for being is to give to others what God has given me, a purpose, a joy, an overwhelming feeling of contentment regardless of circumstances; a reason to go on when all seems lost, a reason to love when you know it will never be returned, a depth of knowing that the creator of the universe, so powerful and masterful, magnificent and caring, loves us and longs to have a relationship with us. So many people ask "Why did this happen?" Why is there so much suffering? This we will never know completely, but we have to trust that the master of the universe has it all in hand. He made us for a specific purpose and our response is all important because it shapes our lives and colours our attitudes.

Reading about the way people have responded and been given the strength to overcome has been a great help. Without that I could never have even started on the search for truth. Albert Schweitzer helped me when I started to make sense of the Christian life. My reasoning was that if a person with that intelligence could believe in Christ it has to be true. Jesus lived and died for us. At that point I only had a faint understanding of what the Christian message was all about. It started me searching, asking endless questions and reading every book I could lay my hands on. There are so many who have lived and died for their faith. There has to be a message in there somehow.

Books on prayer, learning from the Bible and trying to live the life we are taught came much later. There are endless books written on the subject. I shall never become an author – only a follower trying to make sense out of what other people have thought and created.

Giving your life to Christ may sound simple but living it is something you have to grapple with every day. 'Let go and let God' is easy to say but not always easy to do.

Before World War I, I am told that everybody went to church. We do not know how many were there because they enjoyed it or because it was 'the done thing'. So much has changed. The statistics of marriages breaking up have sadly become great cause for concern. Drugs misuse has brought a multitude of other problems in its wake. Both these worrying trends give great cause for concern – I have only added them because I believe that a loving family background is more important than anything else we give our children. My sadness when my own marriage broke up was worse than anything else I have ever experienced.

What do I want to say? I want to say that God has helped me through the hardest times of my life and that his help is available to everybody.

Why do I want to say it? Because I have been given the title 'Not a Humpty Dumpty' and feel the Lord wants me to write a book about the way He has helped me through the anguish of two of our children dying and to help parents who are going through similar experiences, to give them hope and comfort.

Oslo – Norway

What a lovely place to be born! Like all Norwegians I am fiercely proud of my country and very fond of my home town. With skiing from the front door, swimming in the fjord and in the lakes, good schools, excellent theatres and concerts, what more could you wish for? The snowflakes were falling gently the day I came into the world. My parents were delighted and so was my brother, Kjell – a complete little family.

A Norwegian Fjord

However, sadly this only lasted 3 months because my mother went back to hospital and stayed there until I was 2 years old. Medicine in those days was not as advanced as it is now and after a long struggle she died. My father was heartbroken and so was Kjell. I have been told that when Kjell was told that his mother had died he said 'Poor Anne-Lise, she will never know her'. Those were unselfish words from a little boy who had just lost his mother.

For my father there was no time to grieve as he had two children to look after. When I sorted out his papers I found an exercise book containing detailed notes on how to care for a small baby. He cared! So did God who sent a wonderful person to look after us. We called her Dadda. She was a country girl, lively, fun and very loving. Dadda was a committed Christian and prayed for us every day till the day she died. We were "adopted" by her family and spent many happy holidays with them.

When Dadda left to get married her sister 'Ditta' (Edith) took her place. I find it hard to describe her. She was everything you would look for in a kind and loving mother. There was a time my father told me they had plans to get married, but sadly it never happened. When she left I was devastated and took some time to get over it. It was like losing a mother. Coming home from school to an empty house was hard. There was no one to share my joys and sorrows with. She was part of our home and when she left it felt as if one wall was missing. The best escape from sadness was reading. Although I did not know it at the time, that would become very important to me later on in life. The Lord has the whole picture, and used this broken piece for His work.

We lived in a spartan flat on the outskirts of Oslo. My father, brother, my aunt and I shared a bedroom. It

The view from our flat

was cold at times. One morning we found a glass of water frozen solid to the bottom. There was no central heating in those days. None of that bothered me in the least (apart from my father snoring). We had the most important ingredient of all, unconditional love, and I had a happy childhood. The community where we lived was like a village. People were friendly and we came together on special occasions, especially the 17th of May, our national day.

Having been governed by Denmark, and also by Sweden for a while, this marked the day when a constitution was signed declaring that Norway was a country in its own right. We were still united with Sweden until 1905 when King Haakon V11 and Queen Maud came to Norway and became our king and queen. They were warmly greeted and very popular.

It is hard to describe the feeling of being free to run our own country. This is celebrated every year and starts at the crack of dawn with the A-level students driving around in lorries, singing and shouting to wake their teachers; the noise is heard all round the neighbourhood. The teachers are then picked up to have breakfast with the students. Speeches are held, which reminds us of the value of being free and express thankfulness for a beautiful country. It is also a time to remember the people who had made it possible.

Then comes the high spot for the children. Dressed in their best clothes carrying a Norwegian flag they march through the streets of Oslo to the Royal Palace to greet the Royal family, waving our flags and shouting "Hurrah". Our Royal family is much loved by everyone. They make us feel that they are one of us. On 17th May they stand for 2 hours greeting the children as they march past the Royal palace, waving flags and singing or playing in primary school brass bands.

War

On the 9th April 1940 the Germans attacked Norway, and because Norway's defence was very weak it did not take many days before they occupied the whole country. I can still remember the strange feeling I had that day. Nobody had actually told me what was going on, but I picked up from the atmosphere that something momentous was happening.

Preparations were made for people's safety during air-raids. We were not bombed as heavily as other countries, but it was still scary. The Germans told us that they had come to protect us. There were rumours going that Oslo was going to be flattened to the ground. Many people panicked and fled, but my father was not easily frightened, so we stayed put. Nothing happened, and we were better off in our own home.

A few days later Ditta and I went to stay with her family who lived out in the country. The train was packed full of people and their belongings. All of a sudden the train stopped with a jerk. Chaos reigned; suitcases, bags of all descriptions and people were tumbling around everywhere. No one was seriously hurt and no explanation was given.

Shortly after we arrived at our destination a thousand Germans were stationed near the house. One day, some of the soldiers came into the kitchen to warm up and one of them offered me a bar of chocolate. I shook my head. Instinctively I knew that these people were not friends. A tear rolled down the soldier's face. Maybe he had had to leave a little girl at home.

On the 19th December 1942 there was a big explosion in Oslo. The whole town shook. The Norwegian underground movement had blown up the Nazi headquarters.

The cold war went on the whole time. If a German offered you his seat in a tram you were reluctant to take it. Some were put in prison for refusing to do that. Being a child I did not know much of what was going on; my father asked people not to talk about the war in front of me. My brother was eight years older than me. He was great fun and we were very fond of each other, but he was a lively lad and one night when he had been told to look after me he decided to go and meet some friends instead. That meant that I was alone in the flat and I was scared stiff. My father had told me that if anyone should ring the doorbell at any time I was to open the door, as it might be the Gestapo and they would shoot a hole through the lock in the door. Time seemed endless waiting for my brother and father to come home. I was too frightened to move in case someone heard me. Children have such vivid imaginations, and I conjured up all sorts of things in my mind.

One cold winter night my father and I were walking home from the tram. We were warned that a drunk German had taken it upon himself to check people's identity cards. My father and I walked on. There, on the corner of the road, was a German officer waving his gun around. My father told me to go to the police station nearby so off I ran. Then, moments later, – two bullet shots were heard. I started shaking all over. My whole world collapsed. I was sure my father had been hurt. The shots had in fact been aimed at two ladies, but they were too far away so no damage was done. What a relief!

Life during the five years of occupation was very different from the normal run of things. Our primary school became Nazi headquarters and the secondary school a hospital. My brother spent time in the hospital in his old classroom. As there were no students the University was taken over by the schools. No groups of Scouts or Girl Guides were allowed and no competitive sport.

The occupation had its good sides too. People who normally would not be on speaking terms became friendly. We had a common enemy which united our people and, as with any hardship, it made us stronger.

Freedom

The 7th of May 1945. It is interesting that when something extraordinary happens every detail is etched on your mind. I went to the Post Office and was told that the war was over. As there had been rumours of this a week earlier we dared not believe it at first. Later on my brother and I washed up after supper and saw, one by one, Norwegian flags appearing. Each flag was like a nail hammering in the glorious fact that we were free! Oslo went wild, English soldiers came and were treated as heroes. There was such a wonderful atmosphere everywhere; people were singing and laughing.

When King Haakon came back from exile there was rapturous applause and the streets were lined with people welcoming back our very popular king.

It took a little while for things to get back to normal. We were still 'camping out' in various locations until our schools were up and running again.

How we enjoyed being free! I became a Girl Guide and enjoyed that, especially the camps. At an international camp near my home I met girls from other countries for the first time. In our tent one evening a Finnish girl was close to tears. She said 'You are the only people outside our own country who have been kind to us'. They lived near the Russian border and had lost their homes twice when the border was moved. The following year we went to Finland camping in a large forest. Everybody was so kind to us, giving us sweets and chocolates out of their own meagre rations. They said that their parents had told them to be extra nice to the Norwegians because of the support our parents had given the Finns in the war against Russia, sending them balaclava helmets etc. I was invited to stay with a family after the camp was over. They had a lovely chalet by a lake and made me feel very welcome. We went to a real Finnish sauna where we were given the most enormous meal afterwards.

Travelling from the Russian border back to Oslo by myself was an adventure. Every time the train stopped people popped out and came back with all sorts of goodies which they shared with me. I had learnt two Finnish sentences 'I am Norwegian. I do not speak Finnish.'

From Helsinki to Stockholm I went by boat and met young people from all over the world, and had a great time. Then came the train journey from Stockholm to Oslo. It was a long journey but I learnt a lot and met some interesting people. How the world has changed. Today nobody would let a teenager travel that distance alone.

After A-levels I decided to go to Paris as an au-pair girl. It is a great way to learn a language and see more of the world. I stayed with a delightful family with three children, Bertrand aged five, Evelyn aged four and Jean Robert aged 18 months. They were very good teachers as they always told me when my French slipped up. The parents were a lovely couple and we had long discussions at the dinner table, also good for my French.

A short time after I arrived they held big party and asked me to invite a friend. Halfway through the evening I was introduced to one of my own countrymen. We chatted away happily until I realized who he was -my hero – and very famous actor – Thoralf Maurstad. After that I was tongue-tied and very excited. The next thing that happened was a discussion about a painting on the wall. The parents of the people I was staying with were art dealers. There were some genuine Impressionist paintings in the apartment. What intrigued me was that when we were discussing frames, the grandparents confided in us that they had used scrunched up toilet paper to mend one of the frames and then covered that with gold paint!

I enjoyed my time in Paris with so much to see and do, but my greatest enjoyment was looking after the children. The eldest, Jean Robert, felt very sorry for me that I would not have any oysters when I went back to Norway and promised that he would send me a whole case. Who says chivalry is dead?!

Evelyn was a sweet, quiet little girl, Jean Robert very good looking and Bebe adorable and great fun. The children were allowed wine mixed with water for lunch. One day Madame Lavergne was engrossed in a discussion with her husband, and did not realize how much wine she had given her little boy. Suddenly he stood up on his chair and gave a long recital – about some ducks and their antics – we guessed he was drunk – aged 3! I scooped him up in my arms and put him down for his nap – he slept very well that day.

I first got to know my future husband, Robin, in the American Club. It was *the* meeting place for many of the young people from other countries. He was known as 'that funny Englishman' as he has a delightful sense of humour. His dilapidated car, filled to the rafters with students, had sometimes to be persuaded to go, which only added to the fun.

With French bread and wine, I had put on far too much weight and felt very unattractive. We exchanged addresses but I did not think I would ever see him again.

After nine months I went back to Norway via Denmark, where I got engaged to a Dane. One day the doorbell rang. When I opened the door, who should be outside but 'the funny Englishman'!

Robin is in the hotel business and had spent two years at a Paris hotel school. He came to Norway to complete his training and worked at Holmenkollen Tourist-hotel, a beautiful hotel outside Oslo. He perfected his skills in the kitchen and spent three months in reception. We started meeting as friends. As I was engaged to a Dane at the time and as people always leap to conclusions, we kept this quiet – or so we thought. Never will I forget the day when Robin's car stalled in Karl Johan – Oslo's high street. He was wearing a black coat reaching to the ground, a most unusual sight, and driving a vintage car. We were bound to be noticed. I could have died of embarrassment. Oslo has been named the world's biggest small town and smallest big town. You do not attract attention to yourself because there is *sure* to be an acquaintance around who might pass on the news.

Robin stayed in Oslo for nine months. We were still only good friends when he went off to Innsbruck to work and do some skiing. As there was no snow that year he got bored. I have often thought that if there had been snow, my life would have been completely different. When I wrote and told him I was going to Brazil to my brother's wedding he suddenly got itchy feet and came helter-skelter back to Norway. Then came what we in the old days called courtship. After three months we were engaged and were married six weeks later.

Robin's family came to Oslo for the wedding, which was held in a favourite location of ours in Oslo. If Robin was nervous he never showed it. He gave a speech in Norwegian which must have been nerve-wracking for him. We danced till 2 o'clock in the morning. My parents-in-law thought Norwegian weddings were great fun.

Our honeymoon took us through Sweden, Denmark, Germany, Holland and Belgium to England. I was wondering what my new home country would be like and was a bit put out when we drove through Thanet which is as flat as a pancake. I have since grown to love England and consider myself very lucky to have two beautiful home countries.

My husband's family lived in a huge house in Broadstairs. It is called Bleak House; so named after Dickens' novel as he wrote some of his books there.

Coming from a spartan background I had a culture shock. I will never forget the impressive mahogany dining table, complete with silver, crystal glassware and flowers. I was completely overawed, but they are a friendly family and made me feel at home.

Next, my brother-in-law proudly showed me his pet. I thought it was a rat and I am not fond of rats, but as you may have guessed, it was a hamster.

Robin expected to hear about a job offer, which never materialized, so after a few weeks we decided to go to Innsbruck.

We arrived with no job prospects and nowhere to live. Within a couple of days that was all sorted out. Our accommodation was in a farmhouse in Igls near Innsbruck which we shared with the farmer, his wife and their eight children. The floor below served as a home for 10 pigs and our car. Across the road was the local church. The bells chimed every hour and made the farmhouse shake. Robin found a job as a waiter and I was lucky to become a tour guide.

The fact that I did not know the area at all was overcome by my speaking German. I made friends with the drivers, who gave me all the information I needed. I really enjoyed my job. We took parties round Austria and also to Italy and Germany, a great chance to see new places and an opportunity to improve my languages.

Innsbruck is surrounded by majestic mountains and has interesting historical sights. A beautiful river flows through the town. Austria has borders with Switzerland, Germany, Hungary, Czechoslovakia and Italy; a thoroughfare with roads leading to all these countries. I passed my driving test in Innsbruck. You have to know what is under the bonnet and pass a written exam. If there was anything I did not know I pleaded innocence: that I had forgotten the German word for whatever was asked. The examiner came out afterwards and told us we had all passed, but Mrs Collins ought to improve her German!

As I did not have full time work it was a great opportunity to enjoy the sun, swim in a nearby pool and pick masses of wild strawberries. The food for the staff in the hotel where my husband was working lacked both quality and quantity. When we had saved up enough tips we made a beeline for a special restaurant in the town where they served excellent steaks! Nothing since then has ever tasted quite that good.

Richard's Children - Rebecca and Madeleine...

...and Luke

Children

When we came back to England we had no home. Robin needed to finish his training in Hotel Management. We joined Trust Houses (later to become Trust House Fortes). We managed a small hotel in Framlingham, a lovely market town in the depth of Suffolk. It was an excellent opportunity for us to learn how to run a business without having to risk our own money. It was certainly challenging. I found myself doing at least four different jobs; reception, bar, housekeeping and restaurant. As I had very little training it was learning the hard way at times but the customers were friendly and easy to please.

Our first baby, Christine, a lovely little girl with big eyes and long lashes, was born there so we were now a family, complete with boxer dog. Trust House rules said that you had to have someone to look after the baby and my old nanny, Ditta, was delighted to do that. It went well for a while. I fed Christine myself but had little time to bond with her. When I started to realize that Christine began to look to Ditta as her mother we decided that the time had come for us to leave and start to look for a business of our own.

The Pantiles Grill in Tunbridge Wells became our new home. We lived above the restaurant in one room, but everything is fun when you are young and healthy. Our flat eventually became too small so we bought our first house. It was in a beautiful position overlooking the Spa Golf course. It did have one little snag. One summer I counted 50 golf balls in the garden, but nobody got hurt.

Our second baby, Helen, was born 13 months after Christine. She was a cute baby and later had a mop of red curls. The two girls got on very well and had a language between them when they were tiny that only they could understand.

Our eldest boy, Peter was born three years later. He was very easy going. That was a help because life was busy as I still helped in the restaurant. We did have au-pair girls who were mostly very helpful and good company as well.

We did the daftest things. How about buying a house with six huge bedrooms, a butlers pantry, walk-in larder, still room, huge kitchen, grand dining room, lounge you could get lost in and a music room, with very little money to run it? Robin went to the sale rooms to buy beds and came home with the playroom piano!

Marc's children - Paloma and Joseph

How about getting lost in a bluebell wood with two very small children and a boxer dog? Life was never dull.

I was pregnant again and Richard was born in January. With thick snow on the ground the midwife was worried about getting stuck so I had two midwives. Luxury, I have never been so well looked after. It was a hard birth but the baby was healthy. He was a lively boy – full of fun. With red hair, freckles and mischief a favourite occupation he was a challenge, but also very lovable. He is now a father of three and wrote this after his second girl, Madeleine, was born.

A New Hope

My wife had a baby the other day. A little girl named Madeleine Rose who weighed 9lbs 14 oz at birth. Maybe not such a little girl. She was pulled from her mother's stomach and there was a wailing and a rejoicing, weeping and smiles. The surgeon muttered and fussed amidst the clinking of surgical instruments and then I finally declared "It's a girl." She emerged pink and wrinkly, screaming and wriggly, decidedly discontent at losing her snug surroundings. They cleaned her off, wrapped her up and placed her in my arms. She looked up at me with big, blue eyes and took my breath away. No more pain, no more cutting, no more waiting. Just a baby in my arms, as I sat next to my wife while the doctors worked to put her body back together.

The buzz continues but we are already in another world, gazing down at a bundle of humanity who brings us joy just by …..being.

It is a curious and marvellous thing, the birth of a child. A new hope has entered my world. Surely now the trains will run on time, the stock market will only go up, my back ache will recede and politicians will mean what they say. I will smile at the man who cuts me up at the motorway; I will laugh at my plummeting bank statements. The sun will shine, my plants will never die and my wife will always agree with me. Even as I lose sleep I will have the energy to do charity work, visit sick people and clean the house. Those whom I love I will love more fervently. I will be more patient, kind and gracious to my enemies. I will get up early, read Dostoyevsky, remember birthdays and iron. Yes iron!

I am eating strawberries and cream in the front row of Centre Court at Wimbledon during the men's final!

And when my hope is tarnished, when the trains are still late and my back is still aching and I still feel the rough edges of a fallen world, I will try not to lose heart. My plants may wither, my team may lose and my lofty intentions may die within days but some hope will still remain. When I return home from work bleary-eyed with boredom and disheartened, I will peer down at tiny toes and chubby cheeks and I will be reminded of love come down. As I pick her up, I myself will be picked up, sustained. In her vulnerability, I will see my own. In her need, I will be brought face to face with my own frailty, my own need for a father, a protector. And I will be turned once again to my Creator who holds me more tenderly, more securely than I will ever know.

Yes, the birth of a child is a wonderful thing. It gives me hope.

After six years in Tunbridge Wells it was time to move on. The Frimley Hall hotel in Camberley was our next venture. Robin did a great job there and business picked up (after some hard work). We lived in a small flat on the top floor.

Hotel life has many surprises. We experienced everything including a baby born on the landing, fires, burglaries and suicide. We also had many interesting people who came to stay.

The intercom rang – my husband's voice was on the line. 'Ambrosia' he said 'What on earth are you talking about?' was my reply. 'I have served my god.' We did from time to time get famous guests and Stirling Moss, Robin's great hero, called in for a meal.

Working behind the bar was fun too, especially late in the evening when businessmen away from home talked about their families, their hopes and dreams. We heard many funny stories and enjoyed looking after people. Most were nice but of course we had the odd problem. One night a group of Welshmen were having a marvellous time but it was getting rather late (around 2 a.m.). We could not lock up until the last guest had gone to bed. There was a sweeping staircase up to the next floor so to give them a hint that it was time to call it a day I walked slowly up the stairs calling out 'Good night'. What I got was a serenade of 'Goodnight Sweetheart' – not at all my intention. They had missed the point completely.

One evening we had a cadets' dinner. For the first and last time in my life I lost my temper. One of them decided he would like to hypnotize one of his friends. He was laid flat out on a table and went into a trance. What the 'hypnotizer' had not learnt was to gently bring his friend out of the state he was in. When the cadet woke up he grabbed a glass of red wine and sloshed it right down our very expensive wallpaper. As if that was not enough they got hold of a pushchair belonging to a family staying with us and tried to wheel a friend in it. That is when I exploded and dressed the lot of them down. They came up to me later on and apologized. No hard feelings, they were young and full of fun and due to drink somewhat out of control. As I had never lost my temper I was quite overcome and kept on saying to myself 'I did that' feeling quite proud.

Robin was always forward looking. He did not like the thought of the children ending up spending their free time in the town's coffee bars. We found a lovely hotel in the New Forest. There was plenty of room to build a house, and he suggested I might like a log house made from timber imported from Norway. It was exciting having a house built. The men who built it were so friendly and helpful. They bent over backwards to please so when we moved in it was not a house – but already a home.

The New Forest is a special area of outstanding beauty and with a unique character. It was established as a royal hunting preserve by William the Conqueror in 1079. Many of it's traditions remain. Commoners still leave their ponies, cows and sometimes pigs to graze on the Forest.

I love trees, especially the beeches with their delicate green leaves in spring and vivid colours in the autumn. Once the leaves have fallen you can see the intricate shapes of the branches. God is an amazing creator and nothing man can produce comes anywhere near the perfection you find in nature. The myriads of wildflowers come back every spring. I am always excited when I see the first ones appear. Spring speaks to me about the Resurrection. It is like a new miracle every year. Who would think that from the dry, grey branches you see in winter would come the multitude of fresh green leaves. Without the evidence in front of us of Jesus, we could doubt the accounts of him rising from the dead as much as we might doubt the return of spring if we had not seen it every year. Thank you, Lord, for this yearly reminder of your love for us.

Swan Green, Lyndhurst in the New Forest

It is fun having animals around, but not quite so good when they invade your garden. Pigs are sent out in the autumn to eat the acorns as they are not good for the ponies. Four of them decided to use our garage as their bedroom. They were clean and tidy, which was a blessing, but they are fond of bulbs. I did not want to risk them eating our lovely spring flowers so I had the garden made pig proof.

Brockenhurst College is the venue for The New Forest Bible Convention. It lasts for 3 days and draws large crowds. The teaching is excellent and we enjoy the fellowship there, but it mainly attracts people who are Christians already. I can't help thinking how great it would be if every other year we could have outreach at the same scale. There is such need for Christ and his teaching in our society. The statistics are frightening Relationships outside marriage have become the norm, the number of teenage pregnancies is rising, violence in schools is widespread, and drug addiction leading to crime does not seem to diminish. These are some of the problems which I believe good Christian teaching from an early age would help to prevent.

I went to the doctor thinking, great, if it is, and great if it isn't. It was – nine months later Marcus was born. He had the best start in life anyone could wish for sleeping out in the garden in fresh air with an apple tree for a mobile. When I took him into the village there were always people smiling at him so he had a very sunny nature. The whole family adored him. It all seemed too good to be true – five years later disaster struck.

Christine

Christine

Our eldest daughter, Christine, was a fun-loving girl with a great appetite for life. As soon as one event was over she was preparing for the next. Being the eldest in the family she took good care of her sister and brothers. One day she told me that if anything happened to me she would take care of the family. That was very kind and thoughtful but to me that seemed too big a sacrifice as I wanted her to have a life of her own and reach her full potential.

Christine looked up to her father and he adored her. A psychiatrist came to see us the day after we had the news of her death. He told me that my husband would never be the same again and he was right.

Christine was filling in time before starting a secretarial course in Winchester. Having done a certain amount of sailing with her father she jumped at the chance when she was offered a trip across the Channel.

To earn some money she worked at a shipyard in Lymington where she met Timothy Jackson. He was an experienced sailor. When he rang and offered Christine a trip across the channel I was delighted for her. My husband went to see them off, taking Christine some of his warm clothes. He was the last to see her alive.

It was my youngest son Marcus' fifth birthday. He was all excited waiting for his daddy to come home for lunch. The doorbell rang and outside stood the most sinister man I have ever seen. It was Timothy Jackson's father. 'Christine and Timothy are lost at sea' he said. At first I would not believe him. There had been no storms reported so we had not been concerned about them. 'Bits of boat and an uninflated life raft have been found' continued Mr Jackson. It was then that it hit me. It was true, we had to face facts.

Angels looked after Marcus for the next 20 minutes. He was waiting for his birthday lunch and would normally be with me but he stayed right out of sight. He had no idea that he would never see his big sister again.

My husband came home and he was devastated by the news. Ever a man of action, it did not take him long to organize a flight to Dover where the rescue operation was in full swing. With the help of radar they were able to pinpoint the location where the boat went down. The RNLI went out to look for them but found no trace. A few days later there was a report on TV showing the radar of a big tanker colliding with the 'Scamperer' – the boat Christine and Timothy were on. Prince Charles was in the area at that time on board HMS Bonnington and also searched, but there was no sign of them.

27

The birthday party went on – there was no time for tears. When the guests had gone our dear friend and vicar came to see me. We went to a quiet part of the house and sat down. He started talking and gave me a picture of a distant shore – and all of a sudden I stood up and said 'She is happy now and we will meet again'. That gave me confidence and strength to support the family in the difficult days ahead. It was also a great comfort that so many people were praying for us.

A week later I felt a bit tired and lay down on my bed. I opened the Bible at Corinthians 13, that beautiful passage about love. I was led to read on – and to my amazement 1 Corinthians 15 spoke straight into the situation I was in. It gave me the best comfort possible. It reads in verses 15 – 21 *'but tell me this – since we preach that Christ rose from the dead, why are some of you saying there will be no resurrection from the dead? For if there is no resurrection of the dead then Christ has not been raised either. And if Christ was not raised, then all our preaching is useless. And all we apostles would be lying about God for we have said that God raised Christ from the grave. But that can not be true if there is no resurrection of the dead. If there is no resurrection then Christ has not been raised. And if Christ has not been raised then your faith is useless and you are still under the condemnation for your sins."* It was another confirmation that Christine was (and is) in safe hands

As Christine died at sea, we could not have a funeral, but held a memorial service a month later. The church was packed and the men from RLNI stood guard. It was a service of dignity and faith. We had planned it together with the family of the man who went down with Christine and we had no problems agreeing on the order of the service.

When everybody had gone back – the children to school and our relatives back home it was the time for me to go through grief. My initial reaction when I was given the conviction that she was happy and that we would meet again, was that any sadness I felt would be self pity. I had not learnt that grief is part of life.

It was first thing in the morning when it hit me. No, it was not a bad dream; it was true that we would never see our lovely daughter again in this world. She was outgoing and the house was a meeting place for all her friends. We missed that too. Andy, her boyfriend came to see me often. He was distraught and it took him a long time to get over his loss.

It was our past – she was at an age when she would leave home but it was his future and we were very concerned for him.

There came a time when I needed to be on my own – a very personal time that could not be shared with anyone. It was like going down a deep, dark alley and after reaching the bottom slowly emerging into light.

Their birthdays and the anniversaries of their leaving bring back memories of them. Time does heal, but you never get completely over it. On Christine's birthday, Robin sends me one red rose for each year she would have lived. He suffered so much. It made him realize how much he loved his children. He wrote a beautiful letter to our surviving children which they treasure.

My faith has become so real through what has happened to our family. When all the support of family and friends had died down, I went through grief on my own with the Lord. He gave me all the comfort I needed. He is there for all of us – we don't even have to ask, just confide in Him when life gets rough. He does pick up all the pieces and lovingly puts them together. Just like the pottery which is made stronger by being glued together again you emerge as a stronger person.

The Lord never promised us an easy ride. He had nowhere to lay his head. But he invites us to come when we need him. He says 'Come to me all you are heavily laden and I will give you rest'. He will never disappoint you.

My Christian Journey

My Christian journey started when I was very young. My friends next door were missionaries and held meetings – special ones – for small children. I loved going to their flat. They were always such a happy family and treated me as one of their own. There I learnt my first Bible stories about God's love for all his creatures. Their youngest son was my special friend. We went to Sunday school together. It was a long walk from home. The teacher was lovely. She lived out God's love in her teaching and the way she cared for us.

When we grew beyond Sunday school age there was a long gap. We had little teaching at school. The Christians in my class were puritanical – no dancing, no cinemas, no makeup – all the things that are fun at that age. I did go on an Easter holiday with them and asked many questions but they were not able to give any answers that I could understand.

At the age of sixteen I was confirmed, but the preparation was not very helpful. I agreed to be confirmed to please my father.

It was not until I had my fourth baby that I started taking an interest. I had, after all, had four children christened and had promised to give them a Christian upbringing. So out of duty we started going to church regularly. We moved to Camberley in Surrey. One Sunday morning a notice was given about adult confirmation. Somehow I felt that notice was for me. Although I was confirmed in the Church of Norway, I just wanted to find out more.

The teaching, which was more like a discussion group, was excellent. We were helped to think and give our honest opinion. What made the deepest impression on me was that we were not expected to accept the whole Bible. So began the search for truth. I had a long journey of ups and downs, met many interesting people and read a number of Christian books. My husband was not a believer which was good for me as he asked difficult questions that made me think through many issues more deeply.

I had still not made a personal commitment until my youngest son, Marcus, was born. A friend, Davena, had been very helpful. She gave me a booklet which suggested that you could take out 'a family membership', meaning that you could pray for the whole family to become Christians We spent one morning a week talking through all the issues I found difficult to understand and that was a great help. I was now seriously searching and read every Christian book I could lay my hands on. Two of my sons are now believers and one of them is going into full time Christian work.

My sons preferred to go to a Baptist church and as I had 'itchy' feet myself I welcomed the opportunity. The liturgy in the Anglican Church did not at that time seem sincere to me. We found the Baptist church very friendly, the teaching stimulating and the music lively. There was a mixture of old beautiful hymns and new songs making the worship meaningful and enjoyable. House-groups with lively discussions helped my faith to grow and I was baptized – making a public commitment to follow Christ and the teaching of the Bible. I have found that very hard at times but rich are the rewards; the love that passes all understanding, the fellowship of a family that stretches right round the world, the forgiveness for all my sins, the security of knowing that I am accepted just as I am.

We have been given instructions to spread the good news. It is not an optional extra, yet I lack the courage to tell people about it. Through my 18 years of Christian bookselling I have read many books and I know I am not alone in this struggle. Christians through the ages have battled with similar feelings. We can draw strength from knowing that they have succeeded in overcoming failures and setbacks.

I also get the mountain top period when I am given a lift beyond description. We have a beautiful world to enjoy and I love the way God shows us his care and concern. The best antidote to depression is taking the time to immerse yourself in the beauty of creation – be it a flower created with infinite care or whatever inspires you most. It stills your being and opens up a deeper perspective of His love and care.

Doubt is a problem everybody has at times but Jesus has made himself very real to me, which has helped me through the difficult periods of my life. I am still searching for answers to many questions. Christian books are a help but no two people are alike. I find prayer and Bible study helpful, in a group or on my own.

Like most people I find the suffering in the world difficult to understand. How can a loving God let all this happen? So many starving children, so many abused and neglected. There is no perfect answer to that. We have been given free will. It would be very boring to be puppets. Natural disasters, the answer I have been given is that people should not live where there they know this can happen – I find that a poor excuse – the children had no choice. The only reason I have found to make sense comes in the book of Job when God says 'Where were you when I laid the foundations of the world?' You are a very tiny part of the big whole and think you can understand it all!' I know the Bible is true and I have experienced God's love in so many ways, so all I can do is to trust that He has got it all in hand.

I find *"Trust in me and do not lean on your own understanding"*, (Proverbs chapter.3 v.5,) a very comforting quote but we have been given a brain and must use that to the best of our ability. As long as we believe that He is in charge and ask Him to take control the understanding comes bit by bit at the time that He has ordained. No doubt everybody has experiences of certain words or passages becoming more important and helpful from time to time. Sometimes it can be a hymn or part of a reading.

In quietness and trust shall be your strength

Such a simple way to hand over our day to someone who knows us better than we do ourselves. Relying on Him is even stronger. You can put your full weight on Him and stop worrying about whatever is troubling your mind.

My Christian journey goes on. I could not live any other way. He gives me the strength I need, and the conviction, that all will be well. 'Living through Grief' is a little book which came into my hands 3 months after Christine died. As everything was still fresh in my mind I could see how true to life it was. It is very practical and takes you through the various stages of grief. It starts with shock and goes on to numbness. I can still remember when the anaesthetic wore off. You also have to work through painful memories, but get pleasure from remembering the good times you had together. Then comes a time when you feel you have to be on your own to work through and accept what has happened. Tears are a great help and very necessary. They help release the tension. I can still remember crying 'Thank you Lord for tears'.

After we have lived through the various stages of grief we come to the final phase – having accepted the loss you learn to live again. This is very well explained in 'Living through grief'.

I believe in angels. Do you? Not the fluffy big wings kind, but people who appear and help you out of a dangerous or difficult situation.

My daughter-in-law Bettina and my son Richard came to England to explore the possibility of Richard becoming a part of Damaris, a Christian organisation. While they were with me, Bettina had a call from Los Angeles where they live. She was told that two of her relatives had been in an accident. They were driving along on a Sunday morning around 5 a.m. when the driver fell asleep. The car hurtled down a precipice tumbling over and over. Behind them was a car with two firemen inside. They saw what happened, ran down to the accident spot and promptly pulled the passengers out. The next moment the car went up in flames. Only firemen could have coped with that situation. God's hand was at work.

The reading from 'Word for Today' for that day could not have been more apt:

There is a stage at which you don't even know you have been chosen, only God knows. He told Jeremiah *'Before I shaped you in the womb I knew all about you.'* (Jeremiah 1, v5). You didn't die in that car accident because His hand was on you.

One evening at dusk I was coming home from a walk in the Forest. When I crossed the road I fell flat on my

35

face. Cars were coming from both directions when two ladies appeared from nowhere and stopped the traffic. As I was wearing dark clothing the drivers would not have seen me. Guardian Angels – I think so!

There have been many highlights where the Lord has shown me how much he cares. Direct answers to prayers are always exciting. One Sunday when I could not get to church I decided to listen to a tape of The Revd. Bill Welch speaking on 'What would you like Jesus to do for you?' Much anguish went into my prayer asking the Lord whether He wanted me to write that book I have been dreaming about for years. The answer was "Yes, but you must do your bit. It requires dedication and hard work. Are you prepared for this?' It was wonderful to find out that I have the Lord's blessing and that He will be there for me when I need help (which is all the time). THANK YOU!

When Bettina was in labour for 40 hours I was praying for her and was led to my little book called 'Why fear?' 'Have patience. Your prayers are heard, your hope *has* materialised.' That was a tremendous comfort and a few hours later Rebecca was born weighing 10lbs and a healthy, beautiful baby. Bettina took a while to recover as she had to have a caesarean but had no real lasting problems. A very happy outcome!

Two burglaries have been 'healed'. The first was very frightening as I actually saw the burglar. Around 2 a.m. I was disturbed by noise. Having learnt from hearing a young burglar on the radio that it is a good idea to make a sound as – surprise, surprise – intruders do not want to be caught, I made a sound by flushing the loo. There was still noise around so I called out to my lodger, John, and a stranger came out of his room. He fled when he saw me and I dialled 999 double-quick. The police were very helpful and reassuring and stayed on the line with me until the officers reached my home. By then the burglar had fled but it was reassuring to have the officers on the premises. They took a statement and then left, leaving me on my own. The thief had come in through louver windows which had to be left open to the world for the forensic scientist's inspection the next day.

First I dropped on my knees and said thank you for helping me through a scary situation. I then looked round for a way to make a noise in the room in case anyone else had the idea of a night visit. My eyes fell on a cassette which I popped into my tape recorder. To my amazement it started with a prayer of protection, and went on to speak straight into the situation I was in. Sheer relief went through me and thankfulness to God for caring that much. It gave me the feeling that He knows all about us and is eager and willing to help.

The second burglary was harder to take. Coming home after a day at work I found my office knee deep in papers. A burglar had got in and ransacked the house for valuables.

My bed was covered with jewellery boxes and anything else he could find. What a mess! The jewellery was partly treasures my youngest daughter had left me the day she took her own life. It took time to come to terms with that.

A couple of months later my lodger was strumming his guitar. I was weeding our flowerbed and heard him play:

Lord, you are more precious than silver
Lord, you are more costly than gold

Lord, you are more beautiful than diamonds
And nothing I desire compares with you.

Warmth went right through my body and I was healed. I have the memory to treasure of Helen's love for me - no burglar can ever take that away.

After my youngest son was born I was feeling very weak. The fact that I was almost beyond child-bearing age and already had four children had taken its toll on my body. I went to lie down on my bed and was gasping for breath. In this state I thought my last hour had come. I prayed the Lord's Prayer and handed over my will to God. If he were to take me, he would also find people to look after my children. My eyes searched the walls for a Cross but I did not find one. It was sad not to be able to say goodbye to the family, but I was completely resigned and at peace. The next thing that happened was that my son came into my bedroom with his children's Bible wanting to show me something. This got me out of the state I was in. That year I had my most precious Christmas present ever. On a piece of cardboard Christine, my eldest daughter, had managed to mount some blue material on a piece of cardboard and she had embroidered a Cross with an angel kneeling next to it. When I opened that present, two tears shot out of my eyes. Little did we know then that Christine would be with Jesus and the angels so soon? When she died my husband had the picture framed for me.

One summer my husband, our youngest son Marc, aged 18 months, and I were in the South of France. We had hired a sailing boat and were moored in Juan les Pins on the Cap d'Antibes. There were lots of things to be done to the boat before we left harbour, so we overlooked a very important detail - the gas was still on. Not prepared for the sailing conditions in that area and how quickly they can change we were in for a big surprise. From a wind Force 3 we encountered Force 8 as soon as we came away from the shelter of the harbour. I was feeding Marc when my husband asked me to take the tiller while he reefed the sails. So with child in one arm and the tiller in the other I coped, but only just. I was relieved, to say the least, when my husband was free to take over.

Marc and I slid into the cockpit and he fell asleep – or so I thought. Edging my way along with him in my arms I made my way to the bow where we lay down. A few minutes later my husband took a quick look into the cockpit. 'The gas is on' he exclaimed. My handbag was lying on a table which had a drawer on one side. My handbag had slid down to the cooker and turned the gas on. Whether this had caused Marc to look as if he were asleep we shall never know. When we reached Antibes I drew a sigh of relief. We discovered that the dinghy had been wrenched off – an indication of the strength of the wind.

When we got back to England our good friend who had been looking after the house while we were away asked what we had been doing on the Saturday. That was the day when this rather frightening experience had occurred. They told me that they had been worried about us and had been praying all day for our safety. Prayers were answered yet again.

I have had a number of experiences which I feel are not for me alone, but something I should share with other people. They happen to encourage us all. God shows us that he is interested in all our activities and shows his concern in a multitude of ways. People often brush them off as coincidences – I prefer to call them God incidences.

One night I was tossing and turning in my bed (sometimes I have a battle with my bedclothes and the bedclothes always win).Sleep just would not come so I decided to try a form of meditation taught by our pastor David Dewey. I pictured a peaceful scene on the river in Oxford. The boat we were in was gliding slowly down the river bordered by weeping willows. Jesus was punting and I was completely at ease. After a while we came to an island where we moored and went ashore. Jesus sat down and started teaching and I was sitting at his feet – soaking it all in. The boat then came to my mind – I was supposed to try and sleep – so I went to lie down in the boat. I could faintly hear voices of other people coming to listen to Jesus and then I drifted off to sleep.

A few days later I went shopping in New Milton. I was tired and decided to go and have a coffee in a coffee shop where I had never been before. Sitting down at my table I glanced up on the wall in front of me. There, was a picture, describing the scene in my dream. I had to buy it! It reminded me of how faithful God is – His attention to detail never ceases to amaze me. The picture is now on my wall.

Helen

Helen

I was giving my youngest son a bath when the phone rang. When I answered there was a very worried voice on the line. 'I am afraid your daughter is not very well' said the manager of a mountain hotel in Norway. Helen was working there as a chambermaid in order to learn the language. 'She has been behaving most strangely. To begin with she was working a lot harder than anyone else but in the last few days she has got some strange ideas in her head. She thinks that she has supernatural powers'. These were all symptoms of schizophrenia, but we did not know that at the time. A few minutes later the phone rang again 'We can't find her. She has gone out into a raging snowstorm without an overcoat' the manager told us. You don't last long in those conditions. My heart missed a beat. Would they get to her in time? To our great relief they rang again later to say that she had been found.

It was obvious that we needed to get to her as soon as possible. We had good friends who came to look after Marcus and took the first plane to Oslo, where we hired a car to drive up to Tyin where Helen was working. We got there in less than 24 hours. When she saw us her face lit up. 'You know who I am, don't you Mummie' she said. "Yes, you are my daughter" I said. Her face fell. She had been looking everywhere for her identity, even emptying a jar of face cream. Her room looked like a tip. She had smashed everything in sight including her alarm clock as 'killing time' was one of her symptoms.

We eventually managed to persuade her to go to bed and the next day took her to the local doctor. He strongly advised us to get her home. This we did. My husband and I had no trouble communicating during this period. He is first class when something needs to be done. Later on Helen's illness became a stumbling block, as our attitudes to the way we should handle the situation were very different.

The day after we returned home, the local doctor came and spent three hours with us. By then, due to lack of sleep and concern for Helen, I was overwrought and that was not helpful. I did not want Helen to go into a mental hospital. In the end I had to give in and we brought her to The Old Manor in Salisbury. After 3 days she discharged herself and came home.

This was followed by a difficult period. One day you are a normal home – the next a mental hospital with no advice as to how to treat the patient. Many symptoms are similar to character flaws so an extra dose of patience is needed. She did not want to get out of bed in the morning – should you disturb her – and if you did, how could she use her time? She lacked concentration and the drugs she was on gave unwelcome side effects.

After a while she was making plans to go back to Norway. When your daughter reaches a certain age you have little control over her movements. We chose to 'lose her passport' and asked the bank not to issue any travellers cheques. It was unthinkable to let her go off on her own in such a disturbed frame of mind.

A change of scene seemed like a good idea so plans were made for Helen to go to the West Country where her grandparents lived. After four days we had a very worried grandmother on the line. 'Could we please come and collect Helen. She is behaving in a most peculiar fashion.' Robin drove post haste to Tavistock and came back at top speed. Helen tried to open the car door all the way home. She had no idea what was going on.

When Robin and Helen came home she went in through the front door and out through the back. We could not find her anywhere. A search party was started – police, people on horseback, doctors – we were all looking for her. She was found in the local church somehow thinking she was getting married to the devil. It leads me to think that there is a link between the occult and mental illness but how it works I have no idea. Friends tried to coax her to come with them but she refused to budge. They rang me and I jumped into my car and drove down to our local church. Her face lit up when she saw me and was quite happy to come with me. When we got home and she saw all the cars in the drive she looked at me and said 'How could you do this to me, Mummie?' My reply was "You have never had a child of your own. It is impossible for you to know how a mother feels. I need to protect you till you are well enough to do it yourself.' The doctor and the social worker had arrived and told me that she should not come into the house as the symptoms could disappear.

She was sectioned for 21 days – a great relief, as she would then be in a safe place. During that time we had a number of phone calls from her. She was not happy and of course we suffered with her. After six weeks she was moved to a different part of the hospital. On that day somebody there had slashed her own wrists, it did not bode well.

Helen was in hospital for 11 weeks. We were allowed to have her home for weekends. It was noticeable that in the beginning of the drive home her conversation was confused, but after a short while became normal and rational. A psychiatric nurse told me that a mental hospital is the worst place for some patients to be, but necessary for assessment of their need of drugs to develop a normal behaviour.

Helen's doctor said that we should not blame ourselves. She was a schizophrenic, caused by an imbalance in her system which altered her thinking and behaviour. ECT was used at that time, a treatment not all doctors were in favour of. I was asked whether I would permit this, impossible for a lay person to decide, and as the doctor who was treating her told me this was necessary for her recovery I gave my permission. She suffered memory loss after the treatment but this was not permanent.

The National Schizophrenia Society is very helpful. They give the family support and you have the chance to get together with people who have the same problems. I became a co-ordinator and read extensively about the illness, trying to find help as I was completely ignorant in the beginning.

My husband did not agree with this. He felt we should not dabble in a subject we did not know enough about. In retrospect I'm sure he had a good point, but at the time I had to try to understand this complex problem and find out how to care for a sick daughter.

After 11 weeks Helen was discharged from hospital. Again we had no guidelines. To begin with she found part-time jobs but when she became more stable she started up a boutique with a friend selling good quality clothes at affordable prices. Sadly they fell out and ended up selling the business. Big traumas at home – a very unhappy girl.

Helen had a good head for figures. She took a course on bookkeeping and found a job she liked very much. Poor Helen, she was always the unlucky one. Four days after she passed her driving test she had an accident. It was dark and raining, very bad driving conditions. A man walked straight in front of her car. She did not see him and ended up knocking him down. Because of the medication she was on, it did not affect her until about three months later. She was then so distressed she ended up losing her job.

She needed work with no stress and became a petrol pump attendant. I took my hat off to her. It was at times a very uncomfortable job, getting up early in all sorts of weather conditions. The people she was working for were very kind and understanding.

I rang her up one day at home and found a friend answering the phone. 'Helen is not well', she said. When I arrived it was obvious that we needed help. I rang the doctor. He arrived in record time and soon realized Helen had taken an overdose. He rushed her into hospital where she had her stomach pumped out. The 100 paracetemol tablets she had taken damaged her liver. She was sent to a hospital in London specialising in kidney and liver failure. A very good friend came and prayed for her and she recovered.

The Lord was a great strength during that period. I had no time or strength to read the Bible or pray, but a sentence in a Ladybird book I read to my youngest son gave me all I needed. 'From tiny seed he makes a tree – Yet he has time to think of...me?'

A year later Helen had had enough and took her own life. When the police told me, I screamed. Somehow I thought that if I made enough noise I could block it out. It had happened again – losing a child. The whole family was devastated. One of my sons was living in Spain at that time. When we spoke to him on the phone we were crying together – he was very close to Helen and was inconsolable. I had already made plans to go and visit him. My other two sons and I travelled to join him. It was good to be together. We had a lot of support from friends and relatives; nobody could understand why these terrible things had to happen.

A close neighbour lost her son some months before this happened. She gave me this poem which we found very helpful.

Not until the loom is silent
And the shuttles cease to fly
Shall God unroll the canvas
And explain the reason why
The dark threads are as needful
In the weaver's skilful hand
As the threads of gold and silver
In the pattern he has planned.

There is a pattern and a plan which we cannot see or understand. We just have to trust the one who made us all. The Bible tells us 'Lean not on thine own understanding.' I suppose that if we did know everything it would give us too much responsibility.

So Humpty Dumpty had fallen off the wall again and been lovingly put together. The Lord gave me the mental and physical support I needed.

When Christine died, God had given me the conviction that 'She is happy now and we will meet again'. That was exactly what a mother needed to know. Now I see my two girls together enjoying a better life than we can ever imagine!

The worst was yet to come. When my husband left it was as if my whole world had collapsed. I had always felt that at least we had given our children a stable home background. My husband was not a Christian and therefore did not get the help I received.

I tried so hard to share with him, but the enemy was at work and split us up.

We were divorced five years later but have stayed good friends. This is good for the children too, since when we do meet up there is a happy atmosphere. We have three sons and six grandchildren.

I hope and pray that the people who have read my book will be encouraged and turn to God for help. When the need is greatest the Lord is closest, says a Norwegian proverb. I have experienced that many times and it is invaluable.

The Archway

The greatest miracle for me was The Archway. It gave my life meaning at a time when I desperately needed it. After the church service one Sunday, Myra, a member of the congregation said 'The previous pastor's wife and I have been praying for 4 years to have a Christian bookshop in the high street.' I looked straight at her and said 'You will have one in a year.' Those were not my words because I had never had an ambition to be involved in Christian bookselling, but I have loved reading all my life.

Time went on and I had a look at a few properties, none of which proved suitable. The surveys were all unsatisfactory. A Christian friend, Jane Finch, made me an offer of using the back of her Brass shop at a very low rent. At the time I was waiting for a survey and 'put out a fleece to the Lord' (this refers to Gideon, Judges 6, v37-39). 'If this survey is no good I will take Jane up on her offer.' It proved to be useless so that was my clue. When we opened the shop I remembered my conversation with Myra in the church and realized that it had taken exactly a year to materialize.

Mr Bailey of Keith Jones, a big and flourishing Christian bookshop in Bournemouth, was a great help. He gave me time and helpful information about Christian bookselling and also catalogues of the various publishers. These I took home and studied, making a list of the titles that looked suitable. Much to my relief, Mr Bailey approved of my list. I had been reading Christian books for many years, which helped as I was familiar with many of the authors.

I felt 'pregnant' with the shop before we opened. Furniture and stock ordered; would it all fit in and be shown off at their best advantage? Would the books we had chosen be what our customers were looking for? I was helped and strengthened by this: 'Rest in me and trust in me.' That gave me guidance when I needed it most.

A few days after we opened the shop I stood in the middle of the floor, looked around and thought, 'I am standing in the middle of a miracle! I could not possibly have done this on my own.' A deep feeling of peace came over me. God is good and is in charge of everything we think and do.

I had some very good helpers. We all had the same attitude and would only speak about our faith if someone asked. Every morning was started by prayer, giving the day to the Lord and asking for his protection and guidance. It was also a chance to share our joys and our sorrows. The 'camaraderie' we had was very special.

Looking after our customers was the part of our work that we liked best. We encountered such a variety of people and situations. We learnt something new every day and enjoyed the challenge of finding out what the customer wanted and then meeting that need. It was a rewarding adventure, challenging and at times frustrating, as in all businesses things went wrong, but mostly it was a great privilege to serve God and our customers. Choosing stock was the most difficult part of the operation but also great fun, seeing new material coming on to the market. Bibles were the focal point in the shop. I had no idea before we started that there was such a variety of translations, editions and bindings with new ones coming on to the market all the time. This especially took off in Children's Bibles, featuring different artwork and easy to understand texts – all to excite our young readers. On the whole we did very well. Cards, pictures, posters, music, jewellery, children's badges etc., all contributed to the ministry and these were often stepping stones for people to talk about whatever was important to them. We were also agents for Tearcraft, a branch of Tearfund which gives people in the Third World a chance to earn a living and not have to depend on handouts. They produce many beautiful crafts, which are very popular, especially as Christmas gifts.

There is as much ministry in cards as there is in books and helping people choose the right words in a difficult situation is challenging and rewarding. It also struck me that we had a big responsibility because the books people read colours their thinking. We learnt a lot from each other, through the books we enjoyed and the people we came in contact with.

Being a Christian shop we did not have a serious problem with shoplifters but we had a couple of occasions when dishonest people came in. Two young men wanted me to show them some birthday cards and asked me to help them choose. I could not see my office from where we stood and a third man went into it and stole my handbag. The men eventually found a card they liked, paid and left. An hour later, a man rang up and told me my handbag had been stolen. I had not even discovered that myself. He wanted to know my credit card pin number. As I never use it, I did not know what it was. He spun me a story about a special setup between Nat West and Barclay's and that it was imperative to have this information. I got in touch with my son who offered to look for my pin number and give it out when the man rang. After a couple of minutes my brain 'clicked into place'. I rang Barclays and of course there was no such setup.

I let my son know this, so when the thief rang again he did not get the information he wanted. He asked my son what reaction I had to his approach. 'She thought you were a crook' was my son's reply. 'Oh well' said the man 'it was worth a try!' How cheeky can you get!

We had a man who came in every day. His speciality was stealing toilet rolls, the girls' tip money and the odd cake. One day when the coffee shop was empty he halved a cake, took a bit out of the middle and pushed the rest together. I'd had enough of his antics, so the next time he came I quietly told him that he was too expensive for us. He grinned, left and we never saw him again.

One evening I had a phone call from the police. 'I am sorry to have to tell you that your shop has been burgled.' Thankfully it had not been vandalized. There was plenty of proof of breaking in and entering but the insurance company did not pay up as our safe keys were kept on the premises. The safe was well hidden, so we thought no one would find it but whoever was responsible must have watched us taking money out. They got away with £1500. You have to sell an awful lot of books to cover that.

The Christian Booksellers Convention (CBC) is very demanding but valuable and worthwhile. We have excellent speakers and the chance to meet some of the authors. There is an enormous shop floor, giving you the chance to see all the new things on the market. There are also seminars with good teaching about the various aspects of Christian bookselling. It is fun meeting up with old friends. The camaraderie is something you miss when you don't have a chance to go. Being tied to our shops makes it difficult to take in any other Christian conventions, so CBC becomes even more important. We start the day with worship and Bible teaching which is always enjoyable, setting us up for a busy day ahead. There are seminars on all the different aspects of our work and good entertainment in the evenings. Meeting well known authors is always a thrill. The after dinner speaker at the banquet on the first evening is always a person of stature and renowned. On subsequent evenings various publishers invite you to good entertainment and give you a chance to meet some of the authors and artists.

We considered it a great privilege to be part of this ministry. It is very difficult to make any money but that was not my reason for being in Christian bookselling. It is a ministry and we spoke to the world through our window display, the books and all other related material we keep. Our photocopier was very popular, so we had a stream of people coming in who would not normally frequent a Christian bookshop.

There was someone else who did not know a great deal about Christian books - Felix. He slipped in through the back door and made himself comfortable. He was convinced he was in charge. I have to admit that we did not always see eye to eye as he left plenty of evidence for having been around - hair everywhere! Many people came to the Coffee shop because they needed ministry and this was met by the girls who worked there.

Some posters we had made people smile:

FOR GOD SO LOVED THE WORLD THAT HE DID NOT SEND A COMMITTEE

AN EYE FOR AN EYE AND A TOOTH FOR A TOOTH – THAT
WAY WE WOULD ALL BE BLIND AND TOOTHLESS

WHY PRAY WHEN YOU CAN WORRY

IF YOU WERE ARRESTED FOR BEING A CHRISTIAN WOULD
THERE BE ENOUGH EVIDENCE TO CONVICT YOU??

For a few years I was on the committee of the
Christian group of the Booksellers Association. It came
about when I went to an AGM and commented that there
was no one representing the small shops. The Chairman
looked at me and said 'You are it'. It was an interesting
task listening to all the 'big boys' discuss problems and
occasionally chipping in with a comment. I always
considered them the professionals as they were mostly
men with a great deal of experience and know-how. It is
fascinating work to be part of and I am very grateful for
my 18 years in Christian bookselling.

One day I went to post a letter and came back with a
shop. The rent we were paying was way too high so I
decided it would be better to buy a property and pay a
mortgage. I popped my head in at an estate agent's and
was given the details of 11, St Thomas Street. As I put
my foot inside the door it felt right. It was owned by a
charming couple, so we encountered no big problems.
There were two buildings – a shop at the front and a
workshop at the back. The latter had once upon a time
been a fishermen's chapel. That seemed to be another
indication that we had come to the right place.

One Sunday morning I had a bit of time to spare
before going to church. I was weighed down with plans
for moving the shop. We had worked hard trying to plan
the move with paper models of the furniture to house the

books, posters, music, cards and all the other things we sold, but were still uncertain as to how it would work out. The day before I had brought home a little book we could not sell because someone had written in it. For something to do, I opened the book which was called 'Fear Not'. My eyes fell on:

Fear not
You are special
You do belong
You are my responsibility
You are mine
You will hear my voice
For I call you by your name

You are my responsibility – that changed the whole thing. I was completely relaxed. I sat and read a book whilst the removal men emptied the shop.

After 18 years it was time to hand over to somebody else. It took a long time to find a buyer because I insisted on finding a Christian willing to take it on. There were some lovely Christian couples who applied, but the area is very expensive for someone who has not lived here before. Thankfully I did find a local lady who wanted to take it on, and it was a great relief to hand it over to her. The shop is now called The Ark and is doing very well. It has had a complete refit and looks tasteful and inviting. I wish Ginny, the new owner, success in all she has planned for the shop.

Role Models

When I was ten I was given a book telling the story of three famous women: Helen Keller, who helped develop Braille, Madam Curie, who discovered radium, and Elsa Brendstrom who was the Scandinavian version of Florence Nightingale. It made a deep impression on me and has made me realize the influence of good role models. It also shows the importance of how we behave and especially how important that is for children and young people.

I am not in the same league as my role models, but they have helped me a lot, showing by their example that it is possible to go on and to receive strength from the one who will never let you down.

Joni

Joni Eareckson Tada has for many years been an inspiration to countless people. Some will be familiar with her story, but I have been surprised that there are many who are not, so I will tell you just a little bit about her.

From being a lively, sporty young girl she became a quadriplegic. She went diving from a raft and her head struck a solid object. She felt as though a strong current had gone through her body and she was helpless because she could not move her arms and legs. All sorts of thoughts went through her head. She could not breathe under water and was beginning to panic when her sister appeared and was able to support her. Joni was confused because she did not know what was happening to her. She thought that she would be able to go home as soon as the doctors had taken a look at her. Little did she know that it would take two years before she would be well enough to go home. Having to lie on a Stryker frame caused her lack of dignity. The frame could be turned round, which meant that sometimes all she could see was the floor. She raved against God – who wouldn't? but Joni was no Humpty Dumpty. Her determination not to give in despite having to use a wheelchair and with little movements in her arms and legs is remarkable. She has encouraged countless people across the world.

Joni is talented. She paints beautiful pictures holding the paintbrush in her mouth. She has travelled the world over, speaking to large audiences, and has written 32 books in which she puts across Christian teaching in a deep, but also readable way. She serves on numerous boards. For her remarkable achievements, she has also been given many awards.

Living as a quadriplegic is no dance on roses. Having to ask for help for the simplest tasks must be humiliating and tiresome and at times infuriating. That makes it even more amazing that Joni has so much compassion, energy and strength to help other people. Joni is also very artistic and her paintings are much admired.

I was quite overcome when I came back from a holiday and found a letter from Joni. It inspired me to continue writing this book. When they say it is 95 per cent perspiration and 5 per cent inspiration it is not true. In my case only one per cent is inspiration, the rest dogged perseverance. Her courage to go on when all the chips were down is mind boggling. So is the energy, time and strength for all the various activities she is part of.

Her first book, 'Joni', has been published in 45 languages. The response to her book was overwhelming. She prayed about how she could help all the people with similar problems to her own and founded 'Joni and Friends' – to bring the Christian message to the disabled community.   President Reagan and President Bush appointed her to 'The National Council on Disability' and the 'American Disability Act' became law.

Through her work with 'Joni and Friends' she records a five minute program heard daily on 850 stations. I strongly recommend that you buy the latest edition of 'Joni', written 25 years after her first book came out. You will find that a lot has happened in those 25 years – receiving honours from many organisations and living a very active life.

'Joni and Friends' is dedicated to extending the love and message of Christ to people who are affected by disability. She has experienced first hand the love and support of her church and her friends and knows how that has made it possible to surmount the difficulties and live a life radiating His love.

One year, as Christmas was approaching, I had a very negative attitude to it, same story, same songs, everyone scurrying around to get it done by that very important date. It would all be a repetition of Christmases past. That was until I read a chapter in a book written and illustrated by Joni. It was headed 'The Greatest Miracle'. I want to share it with you because it gave me back the awe and wonder of our Creator and I hope it may do the same for you.

The Greatest Miracle

Have you ever wondered what might have been the Greatest Miracle? There are certainly enough from which to choose. Think of the Old Testament miracles like the destruction of Sodom and Gomorrah, the parting of the Red Sea, or the day the sun stood still in the heavens at the prayer of Joshua. Or how about creation itself? A universe leaping into existence at the merest word of the mighty Creator!

Over in the New Testament you could include Jesus turning water into wine, walking on water, quieting an angry sea, or raising the dead. The list is long, the examples are many and I'm sure the debate could go on indefinitely. But, let me propose a miracle in a class by itself...

Consider the fullness of God – the God who set suns and stars in motion, carved out rivers, puckered up mountain ranges, ladled out seas, dreamed up time and space and formed you and me in the womb – the same God who did all these things coming to earth as a baby.

God, the very essence of love and holiness, justice and mercy...the miracle of this God entering history in baby flesh. The very voice which once spoke creation into being, now crying for mother's milk. The eyes of the Ancient of Days that roamed to and fro throughout the galaxies, now new, blurred and teary God...with little pink hands and feet, soft silky hair and fresh dewy skin. What miracle can compare with that?

Shaking his head in wonder, the apostle writes of
the One
Who being in very nature God
Did not consider equality with God
Something to be grasped
But made himself nothing
Taking the very nature of a servant
Being made in human likeness
And being found in appearance as a man
He humbled himself

I don't think there is any question. Those words describe the greatest miracle of all. When you think about it, the incarnation is such a mind-staggering miracle that the rest seem almost secondary.

The very voice that spoke creation into being
Now crying for mother's milk

If we can believe that GOD CAME IN THE FLESH, then all the other miracles are simple. Changing water into wine? Nothing to it! Opening blind eyes? Child's play! Raising men from the dead? No great matter for the Lord Jesus. The biggest miracle of all, the miracle of His birth, makes all the other stunning things that happened seem minor, almost simple.

In the season of wonder and rejoicing over the greatest miracle of all, I join with you in adoration of our God who has come in the flesh. What a miracle!

Come let us adore him!

A Christmas Longing, Scripture Press, 1990. Used with author's permission.

Corrie

Corrie Ten Boom was a living example of how you can go through the most horrifying experiences and not become a Humpty Dumpty.

The Ten Boom family were devoted Christians who dedicated their lives in service to others. Their home was always an open house for anyone in need. Through decades, the Ten Booms were very active in social work in Haarlem, Holland, and their faith inspired them to serve in whatever way they could.

During the Second World War the Ten Boom home became a refuge, a hiding place from those hunted by the Nazis. By protecting these people, Corrie, Betsy, her sister, and their father risked their lives. This non-violent resistance against the Nazis was the Ten Boom way of living out their faith. It led them to hide Jews, students who refused to co-operate with the Nazis, and members of the Dutch underground resistance movement. There were usually 6 or 7 people illegally living in the house. Additionally refugees would stay for a few hours until another 'safe house' could be found for them. Corrie became a ringleader within the network of the Haarlem underground. With a group of helpers, she would search for courageous Dutch families who would take in the refugees, and much of Corrie's time was spent caring for these families. Through these activities the Ten Boom family and their many friends saved the lives of around 800 Jews and protected many of the underground members.

The day came when they were found out. In February 1944, the Gestapo raided their home. They had set a trap and waited throughout the day, seizing everyone who came to the house. By evening 30 people had been taken into custody. Corrie, Betsy and their father were arrested. Three other members of the Ten Boom family were also sent to prison. Although the Gestapo systematically searched the house, they could not find what they really wanted most: Jews. They were safely hidden behind a false wall in Corrie's bedroom. In this hiding place were six people. Although the house remained under guard, members from the Resistance were able to liberate them 47 hours later. The six had managed to stay quiet in their cramped, dark hiding place for all that time even though they had little food and no water. They were taken to safe houses - four survived the war.

Corrie's beloved father, Casper, died in prison after ten days. When he was asked if he knew he could die for helping the Jews, he replied, 'It would be an honour to give my life for God's ancient people'!

Corrie and Betsy spent ten months in three different prisons - the last was the infamous Ravensbruck. The sisters were so courageous that they even thanked God for the fleas. It meant that the cruel wardens kept away as they did not want to be bitten.

Life in the camp was almost unbearable, but Corrie and Betsy spent their time sharing the love of Jesus with their fellow prisoners. They ministered in various ways: listening to the hurting people around them, - caring for the children when the mothers were too ill to look after them and shared their faith. They even managed to hold birthday parties for them.

In the end Betsy's health did not stand up to the cruel conditions and she died. Corrie's heart was broken but she carried on with the work they had started together. Many women became Christians in that terrible place because of Corrie and Betsy's witness to them. Their brother, Wilhelm, was also a ringleader for the Dutch underground and died shortly after the war.

Four Ten Booms gave their lives because of their commitment, but Corrie came home from the death camp. She realized that her life was a gift from God and she needed to share what she and Betsy had learnt in prison.

There is no pit so deep
That God's love is not deeper still
And God will give us the love
To forgive our enemies

At the age of 53 Corrie began a worldwide ministry which would take her to 60 countries in the next 33 years. She testified to God's love and encouraged everyone she met with 'Jesus is victor'. How amazing that she could do that after all she had been through.

She has written a number of books – the best known is 'The Hiding Place' which was also made into a film and later released as a video. Corrie was a woman who was faithful to God and who inspired countless people.

Vic

Vic is a perfect example of what happens in a person's life when you trust God.

Repentance, I have been told, is what happens when you make a complete turnaround. This is what happens when you give your life to Christ. You ask and accept His forgiveness and hand your life over to Him.

Vic did not have an easy start in life. His temperament was that of a lively youngster. He was abandoned by his mother when his father died and was only 15 months when that happened. During the war he was moved from one children's home to another. He was starved of love and got into trouble at a very young age. Stealing was his way of reacting to the situation he was in and he did plenty of that. By the time he was 11 he had given up all hope of getting away from the orphanage. To his delight, a year later he was fostered. At long last a semblance of a normal family life had come his way and for a while all went well. Sadly, he could not stop himself thieving. What made him let down the only people in the world that he loved, he says himself, is for the psychologists to work out. In disgrace, he was returned to the orphanage.

Later, after a long period of surviving homelessness he ended up in prison. One day he was drawn to read a Bible left in his cell by the Gideons. Most of it did not mean anything to him at that time, but when he read of the death and resurrection of Jesus something stirred in him. He fell to his knees and prayed 'God, if you are there, you've got ten days to change my life and if you haven't done it by then you've copped it'. He spent a long time praying. He wept for the people he had hurt.

He was ashamed and had no one to tell but God. The next day he told the Chaplain who was at a loss of what to do next. He sent him 'The Methodist Recorder' and with the help of that and his Bible he became convinced that there was a God who loved him. He wanted to change and the result has been a life spent in service to other people, activity and devotion. A thank you for what God has done for him.

Vic became a student at Spurgeon's Theological College and was ordained into the Baptist Ministry at East Hill Baptist Church, Wandsworth. After leading that church to considerable growth, he undertook the pastorate of Godstone Baptist Church.

In 1977 he became the Executive Director for Evangelism Explosion in Great Britain and five years later was promoted to the position of Director for all of Europe and Israel. In 1985, believing that God was leading him into a wider field of evangelism, and with the help of a number of Christian businessmen, he founded Hope Now. It is an organisation which sets out to preach the gospel and give practical help wherever it is needed. Orphans, street kids, prisoners and the poor have become Vic's passion.

Everyone is important to Vic. After the death of my youngest daughter, he called on and off for a whole year just to say "Hi", to make sure I was OK. That gave me strength. He has preached throughout Europe, Africa and the United States. Vic is also much in demand as a conference and after dinner speaker and he is a good Bible teacher. He has been used by God to reach with the gospel of Christ many thousands of people from every strata of society.

Vic's congregation at Prison 62, Ukraine

A simple way to illustrate the Gospel's message - Vic put on the prisoner's coat and gave him his own!

Hope Now is an organisation I have great respect for. Vic Jacobson, his wife Sue and capable volunteers have helped countless people over many years. The two most important areas are Ukraine and South Africa.

One group in Ukraine made me realize how desperate they are. Having no homes they used wreathes in the cemeteries to build a shelter for the night. When that became too cold they resorted to sewers - what a life for a human being, let alone children. Hope Now gave them the love, homes and care they had been starved of.

The children's institutions were badly equipped, so Hope Now has helped with sanitation, providing new indoor toilets and washing facilities, which were in such a shocking state to say nothing of clothing and health-care. They have also built pre independence homes for orphans so that when they leave the children's homes they do not have to face homelessness as Vic did. Provisions are made for training so that they will be able to look after themselves.

Prison work is another part of Hope Now. The prisoners live in dreadful conditions with no privacy (200 plus to a cell) and horrendous sanitation. Food is scarce and Hope Now has installed bakehouses so they can make their own bread. In Prison 62 they have built a chapel. I was privileged to go to Ukraine with Vic and visited that prison.

What struck me was the expression on the faces on those who were Christians. It is hard to describe the openness and peace they radiated while Vic was preaching. The prisoners were truly glad to see us and gave us beautiful gifts they had made out of wood. Their singing brought me to tears - their deep Russian voices filled the room.

In addition to this, Hope Now has a medical team ministering to all sorts of health problems and started DentAid, with particular focus on cleft palate surgery.

Nothing is too big or too small for Vic. Wherever there is a need he goes all out to fill it. His greatest gifts are evangelism and coming alongside people in all sorts of situations.

South Africa. In my ignorance I thought that the problems of the coloured people were over. Well, that ain't necessarily so – to quote an old song. A school for coloured people had no textbooks; the attitude had been that they would be better off without as they would never amount to anything. Hope Now equipped the school with books and a recreation ground, giving the youngsters somewhere to let off steam.

Vic has also written some good books. His first, 'Prison to Pulpit', is his life's story and well worth reading. It is an 'easy read', written in a style which would appeal to people from different backgrounds' 'Good morning Disciple' is a well written commentary on Colossians which has inspired many people. 'Kindlings' is another book which has helped people to understand and apply the Bible to everyday life.

These are the people that make headlines. There are many more you never hear about, and I would like to introduce you to a few I have had the privilege to meet.

Brian

In writing this, I am drawing upon the manuscript of a book Brian has written (but not yet completed). I hope you will see that despite the hard times he has had to go through he is a great guy, thanks to his giving his life to the Lord.

Brian had a tough start in life. He lived on an estate where there was gang warfare going on and inhumane punishments meted out at school. The youngest of six children, he did not get the attention he craved for at home. He ended up being naughty so that his mother would notice him, and that did not help the situation. She did go up to Brian's school when he had been cruelly treated which shows she cared. On one occasion, the teacher pressed her fingers into Brian's head, spun him round and pushed him out of the classroom while his mother was watching.

Eventually Brian got sick of school. – Punishments included being made to stand on tiptoe with his nose in a circle drawn on the blackboard by the teacher. It was when his toes got tired, forcing him to go down on to the floor, that he received slaps across his hands from eight rulers, tied together with sellotape. Extremely painful.

The punishments he received at school rubbed off on him, and he started being violent at home and in the playground.

Brian's father worked hard but spent much of the money he earned on alcohol. This brought the family near to eviction. His mother saved the day by going out to work canvassing for soap powder. She had a hard life, bringing up six children, and a husband who drank most of his wages. Almost nightly, Brian was woken by his parents rowing. It was not a good background, giving little protection from the bad influences of other children.

At weekends he got up early to meet his friends. They went off to Saturday morning pictures together. The money they had was spent on sweets. They sneaked into the cinema without paying. When they came out they went down to the river and got up to all sorts of mischief such as untying the boats and watching them float away. On the way home they made a game of going into a shop and snatching whatever they could, right in front of the shop assistants, and would then run for their lives. It was not only sweet shops that were a target, but jewellery shops as well.

On Sundays Brian was sent off to Sunday school with his sister. He went in a couple of times, but after that he would leave his sister there and meet her later. They went home together so that he would not be found out. If he had gone to Sunday school at that early age he feels that he would have found the love and happiness he was craving for. Making wrong decisions is something we all suffer from. There was no one there to point him in the right direction.

He got up to all sorts of tricks at school. With a friend he put elastic bands in the oil heater with the result that the classroom was filled with smoke and the whole class had to evacuate the room until it was clear.

Other tricks included putting the blind cord around a chair and hanging it out of the window making it crash into the classroom underneath. He was so incensed by one punishment that he put weedkiller into the teachers' teapot. A friend warned the teachers, so no damage was done, but he nearly ended up in the Magistrate's Court for that. In an art class Brian and a friend were flicking paint across the classroom. His friend was sent out and Brian was next in line. By then the teacher lost his temper and knocked him to the floor followed by the paint. There was paint all over the floor and Brian was rolled in it.

Around the age of 12 he joined the army cadets, which he enjoyed. He learned to play the bugle and went on to become a drummer in the cadet band which led the Basingstoke Carnival. They also showed off their skills of formation marching at local fetes. The discipline did him some good but not enough to put him on the straight and narrow.

With some friends he stole the tyres off a car. They did not know they were being watched by a policeman. He reported them and a police car turned up on the scene. Brian was frightened as he was driven to a detention centre, to an unknown place, not knowing what to expect.

The discipline at the centre was strict. They were woken to the sound of shouting wardens; some of the lads were badly beaten. After breakfast they marched back to the dormitory to change into vests and shorts to run a mile in less than six minutes (or do it again). After this they had to change and go off to the parade ground to do some drill. They all bumped into each other, which made Brian laugh - not a good idea as he ended up being beaten around the head. There was a lot of violence in the centre involving broom handles, buckets and anything else those boys could get their hands on. Brian stayed there for three months. It did him no good as he felt more rebellious after the experience.

Brian moved around a lot staying in bed and breakfasts most of the time. He was drinking heavily and got into fights, losing most of them. In one fight he was 'bottled in the mouth'. Determined to get the two men, he chased after them until he collapsed outside a taxi rank where he was found and rushed to hospital. He lost three pints of blood and received 25 stitches to his face.

Accommodation was a problem. At one time he was living in a big warehouse; it was a squat full of drug addicts and glue sniffers. Brian slept on a mattress thrown on the floor in an office. The warehouse held a lot of stolen cars which the squatters used to drive around in. They stole electricity from a nearby cottage and had loud bands to play at weekend parties.

Brian fell in love and went on to get married. They had two sons but the marriage was a disaster and he found himself on the road again. With no skills to support him, burglary seemed an easy option. He was caught and ended up in Winchester prison.

When he got out he found a new girlfriend and they had a daughter. The problem of Brian drinking and ending up at the police station most of the time did not do much for their relationship. His wife got fed up, left their little girl outside the house and threw all her clothes out of the window.

The little girl was cared for by neighbours. When Brian found out, he was furious, kicked in the back door and smashed up the whole inside of the house. The girlfriend ended up in hospital. That relationship did not last so Brian was on his own again. He was picked up on non-payments of fines and sent back to Winchester prison for a short time.

Brian was seeking happiness but looked for it in all the wrong places. He moved to Bournemouth, where he fell in with bad company. He started smoking cannabis again, as he had done when he was 16, and it was not long before he was snorting 'speed' (amphetamine), and then ended up fixing speed into his arm with needles, taking 'acid' and 'chasing the dragon', which is smoking heroin. That was not enough for him so he mixed 'speed' with heroin and shot that straight into his arm.

To support his drug addiction he was back into burglary and with a friend decided to break into a camera shop. They helped themselves to as many cameras as they could carry, plus an electric typewriter. The police were hot on their heels and after a terrifying chase they were found and arrested. In the morning they were charged with burglary and remanded to Exeter prison. This was a really terrible experience for him. Brian was put in the hospital wing next to the padded cells and given something to eat which was to help him come off drugs. As a result of that he lost his appetite and went down to 8 stone. At night he was obsessed with thoughts of drugs, and could not sleep with the men in the padded cells screaming and shouting. This was slowly driving him crazy, causing him to shout back and smash up his cell.

He was sentenced to one year and sent back to Exeter Prison but not to the hospital wing. Brian met up with an old friend and shared a cell with him. The friend was good at art and challenged Brian to have a go. He really did not think that art was for him as all he could remember from his schooldays was flicking paint across the classroom. The friend insisted and taught him the basics. Brian ended up drawing portraits for the other prisoners of their wives, girlfriends and children, drawn from photos.

When he came out he caught up with old friends and went straight back to the drug-scene. That, plus heavy drinking was bad news, and within four months of his release from Exeter prison he was held for attempted murder. He was in hospital, with three policemen at his bedside, in agony with a broken leg which needed to be plated and pinned. The charge was dropped to grievous bodily harm as the man he had injured recovered.

After six weeks in Dorchester prison he was called into the principal's office and given the bad news that he had been allocated to Dartmoor Prison, about which he had heard many bad things. On arrival he was given a number and prison clothes that were far too big for him, and taken outside in the cold misty air to the introduction wing to receive a dinner from the hotplate. It was then that he had his first taste of Dartmoor. He asked for a slice of bread and was shouted at and threatened with the 'block' (solitary confinement). When he finally got to his bed he felt he had landed in hell.

Help was at hand, although he did not know about it for some time. Another prisoner owed him some money and Brian thought 'There is going to be trouble next time we meet'. To Brian's surprise, after sorting things out between them, he was told 'Brian, you need to come to church'. Brian laughed his head off and said 'Church, that isn't for me, you're joking'. Every Sunday morning his friend called at his cell asking him to come to church. This went on for three months. A kind of friendship was built up between them, so finally Brian gave in to him and went along to the church one evening.

He was sitting in the middle of all the prisoners when a side door opened and a group came walking in with musical instruments. While they were singing, he noticed how happy these people were with their smiling faces and he looked around the room filled with prisoners and thought 'I should be up there with those happy people.' After that he went to church every Sunday and got involved with all the church activities. The prisoners close to his cell and the ones he worked with noticed this and would say 'You are only going to church to get parole.' This used to get to him, as deep down he knew he could not control his life. He knew he had to have the love of Jesus Christ in his heart in order to live a far happier life.

One day, the man who had invited him to church came up to him and asked if he really wanted to hand his whole life over to Jesus. Brian said yes. His friend said, 'Sit down, Brian, put your hands together and repeat these words after me'. This was not easy as there were a lot of other prisoners in the room, but by then Brian did not care. He wanted his hardened heart to be washed through, and filled with the love of Jesus and the inspiration of the Holy Spirit.

This is what happened as he put his hands together and repeated the 'sinner's prayer'.

He had a strange feeling of association as he sat there. Just as he said amen the most wonderful thing happened. He was filled with the Holy Sprit and felt a tingling sensation as if his hair was standing on end.

When he went back to his cell and sat down to write about what he had experienced he had a vision. He felt as if he had been lifted out of a greenhouse, and was looking in through the glass at all the other prisoners. He felt he had a need to go back into the greenhouse to help others. To quote Brian 'This might sound crazy to some, but that is what I truly felt that night'.

The next morning, he felt that he was going to end up a lot happier than the man he was before going to Dartmoor. He had a feeling of hope as he had been given the answers to a lot of his questions about life. Of course he still had problems as he was being transferred to another prison, but those were safely in the hands of God. When he first arrived in Dartmoor he had thought 'This is the end for me – if only I could find a rope ladder.' It was in church that he found the rope ladder which lifted him from sadness to joy – to be given plenty of hope. As far as Brian was concerned, God had not only changed his life but his attitude as well. That does not happen overnight but takes a lot of patience .He was given joy in his heart too and he was experiencing the changes that God wanted him to make. He found himself a much happier person having learnt from his mistakes as in 1 Corinthians 15 v 33-35: 'Make no mistake, bad company corrupts good character. Come back to a sober and upright life and leave your sinful ways.'

It would have been great to be able to say that from then on it was all plain sailing, but Brian met old friends and before he knew what was happening he was on the crime scene once again. He went to a party where there was heavy drinking. The phone rang. It was his friend's girlfriend. 'I'm being raped' she said. His friend drove from Basingstoke to Reading in 15 minutes, kicked the front door in, beat up the guy, tied him up, bundled him into the car and brought him back to the party. He was put in a dark room where he was beaten again; the room was covered in blood. Brian did not take part in the violence. The man tried to escape and was thrown on the floor, beaten again and shot in the chest. The situation was well out of control; it was pandemonium. The man was taken to some woods and left for dead. A farmer found him there and took him to hospital.

Moments later the front door (which had been left on the latch) swung open and 16 Thames Valley CID officers walked in and arrested all the people in the house. Brian was taken out first, passing uniformed police, dogs and handlers to the car park full of police cars. The case came to court. The session lasted from 10 a.m. till 5.30 p.m. The red robed judge was capable of giving three life sentences out of four of those charged. At the back of the court Brian spotted a familiar face. It was an elder from Basingstoke Community Church who had given him a lot of support whilst he was worshipping in that church. Brian was released on bail after three months with a curfew to report to Basingstoke Police Station twice a day.

He was staying with his mother at the time and returned to the church. He felt it was a big mistake leaving God's side, thinking he could do without Him in his life.

When the case came to court members of his church were there praying for him. He was told he was free to go as he had already done three months on remand.

The following verses became very meaningful to him. Proverbs 3 v. 1 – 8 reads:

My son, do not forget my teaching,
But keep my commands in your heart
For they will prolong your life many years
And bring you prosperity.
Let love and faithfulness never leave you;
Bind them around you neck,
Write them on the tablets of your heart,
Then you will win favour and a good name
In the sight of God and man.

Trust in the Lord with all your heart and lean
not on your own understanding.
In all your ways acknowledge Him
And He will make your paths straight.

Do not be wise in your own eyes
Fear the Lord and shun evil;
This will bring health to your body
And nourishment to your bones.

When Brian came out of prison for the last time, he got into trouble through meeting old mates. He moved from Basingstoke to Southampton to get away from these people.

Then at last he found the happiness he had been searching for. He met Amanda, a lovely girl. They had a lot in common. Amanda had also had a troubled beginning. She wanted to come to church with Brian, where she gave her life to the Lord and was filled with the Holy Spirit. They both felt it was the best thing they had ever done.

They got married in 1990 and Brian says it was the best wedding you could wish for. It was a great day for them both after all the trauma they had suffered .He says that Amanda looked like an angel and they were both happier than they had ever been. After a period of experiencing housing problems they were offered a three bedroom flat in Ocean village. They now have three children, the eldest two from Amanda's first marriage.

City Life Church in Southampton has been very supportive, especially a man there called Jo who became like a father to them and a grandfather to the children.

In 1992 Brian told the church about his vision from God to start a ministry to prisoners and their families. He was told he was not yet ready, as he was still young in the faith and had a lot to learn. In 1994 he got the go ahead and started Door UK. Part of its mission Statement is to be an expression of Christian love, without thrusting the gospel on anyone. Brian attempts to demonstrate rather than to preach the good news of Jesus Christ.

The organisation has now grown and is in contact with many churches.   It has stopped prisoners re-offending and many have become Christians.   Brian has not got a car but still travels and visits people in prisons around the country.   He is a shining example of faith in action.

Hannah

I had been praying for a companion, male or female, for a long time. My house is ideal for having a lodger. It is built in two halves so there is plenty of breathing space. Hannah was looking for somewhere to live, and was happy to come and share the house with me.

We have a relaxed relationship and share our joys and our sorrows.

Hannah was brought up in a Christian home and is one of eight children. Being the fifth child of eight her mother did not have much time for bonding with her as a baby, which led to her feeling undervalued and lacking confidence. She had plenty of Christian teaching at church, Holiday Bible School in the summer, Christian Fellowship holidays and missionary links. The Bible with Scripture Union notes helped her learn to read.

Life was not always easy and reading became an escape route for her.

Music was always part of family life for Hannah. Her parents enjoy singing; all the children had piano lessons, and some played other instruments. Hannah has a lovely voice, which was trained from an early age, and she sang in several choirs. This is significant because she chose to go to a concert one birthday, and there responded to what Christ had done for her.

Recognising God's provision for her in many practical ways as a youngster, she has since had many occasions to see Him touching her life in emotional, intellectual and spiritual ways. She has had to change her rebellious attitudes, often through learning the hard way. Her marriage broke down after five years, a trauma which

God has used as a healing and sharing opportunity over the last 15 years.

Her work training began at home with weeding, somewhat reluctantly, then a few weeks on a local market garden one summer taught her the joys of planting and harvesting on a large scale. After difficult years in an independent school for girls, she was introduced to the Good Gardeners Association, and was thoroughly taught the principles and practices of organic gardening.

Hannah became a fully-fledged gardener. She went to Askham Bryan College, for two years, sandwiched with six months at Derby and six months at Windsor Great Park. Management techniques and landscape Design were also part of the Higher National Diploma course. Positions held included those of Head Gardener and Assistant Park Manager; several ending abruptly after only brief employment, because of misunderstanding and poor communication. The different jobs she had taught Hannah how people relate to creation, and how necessary it is to care positively for each type of environment. The loss of secure status made her much more dependent on God.

Sadly, manual work strained her arms to the extent that she could no longer work as a full time gardener. She turned to care work in the community, and is now working in a local home for the elderly. Hannah has much to give to other people. I am fortunate to have her as a companion and friend.

She is Not a Humpty Dumpty.

Before Christmas 2003 Hannah was told she had cancer and was very quiet. Contact with her family led to a prayer chain being formed around the world. Local friends and our church folk began to pray too. She had a mastectomy on a Tuesday, came home on Thursday and walked down to the village (half a mile away) on Friday. We were all very concerned about her, but she came through her ordeal with flying colours. That did not mean that she was without distress, but her shining faith helped her through.

Next on the list, chemotherapy was another hurdle. Within a short time she lost all her beautiful hair. She had a wig at the ready and looked very glamorous. The wig was hot and uncomfortable, so I soon got used to seeing her around the house either without it or sporting an array of caps and hats. We had many laughs about this. She returned from chemo very tired, but went out to work the whole time, as well as leading a Brownie pack, an amazing achievement.

Radiotherapy came next. She had to report for that every day for a month. The church was very supportive and people took it in turns to drive her in for treatments. Then came the longed for appointment at the hospital. She came home, beaming with pleasure, no more appointments for six months.

The treatments had worked. She was free of cancer. We celebrated in style going out for a sumptuous meal, and she has been praising God more openly ever since.

Kate

Kate is the closest to a saint I'm ever likely to meet. I got to know Kate some 12 years ago when she came to my shop to buy cards for her friends. There was something very different about her and in the beginning I could not work out what it was. She never looked straight at me and that puzzled me. When the shop moved to the other end of the town she gave us a lovely plant and started coming to see us – always with a packet of biscuits, offering to price our cards for us. Right from the beginning I developed a soft spot for her and one weekend she came to stay at my house. That is when I found out the background to her reluctance to look straight at me. She told me about her childhood when she experienced deep trauma.

Kate was one of four children. She was raped by one of her brothers when she was eight years old. There was very little money in the family. Father left and her mother brought up the children on her own. Kate was sent to beg for clothes in the neighbourhood. In return they asked for favours she was too shy to tell anyone about. Her mother was cruel and Kate could not wait to leave home.

To earn a living without education proved difficult. Kate found a position as a live-in carer for an old lady. It was like leaping from the frying pan into the fire. The lady took pleasure in hitting, punching and pushing her. Kate did not know what to do. She was not a Christian in those days and had to earn a living somehow. When the old lady died she took another position as a carer, but she was no better off as the lady she looked after was selfish and cruel. How she stood it I don't know.

When Kate moved to London our friendship became deeper. She lived in a top floor flat in the East End of London. Nowhere have I been made more welcome. There was a poster at the entrance saying 'WELCOME ANNE-LISE' and around my bedroom more posters, bed socks, cuddly toys and hot water bottles. She could not do enough for me and I felt very spoilt.

The focus of Kate's conversation is always the Lord. She lives and breathes the gospel and tells me of all the marvellous things He has done in her life. We come from different backgrounds but have this in common – to love and to serve the Lord

Kate is no Humpty Dumpty.

Jesus transformed her and gave her a special ministry, to look after the dying. An impressive award was given her when she left the scheme. It states that she exceeded the standard of care involving 882 visits, passed the course on manual and client handling techniques and contributed to the global intercession for those with life-threatening illness.

Kate now has a job which is a lot more fun but is also challenging and demanding. People with Aids have little energy to look after their children and a 'granny scheme' was started. This puts Kate into situations which need a great deal of tact and understanding. She loves all the children and makes sure they have some fun. At the same time she is teaching them good behaviour, respect for God and for other people.

Her shining faith is an inspiration to everybody she meets and I feel privileged to be her friend.

Kate gets all she needs from God. He is her 'reason for being' and she gives herself totally to him and to his work. She shines in dismal surrounding – living in the East End of London – and works unreservedly to give comfort and help to people in need. She loves the children she is looking after with an affection and energy that is hard to understand as she had so little herself as a child. The Christian message is sometimes made too complicated. The most comforting sentence in the Bible to me is 'Unless you have a mind of a little child you will never enter the kingdom of heaven'. This is an attitude we both have and Kate lives it out in her complete and faithful service to the Lord.

Kate has twice been chosen to go to Uganda to an International Prayer Conference. What an honour! Where does she get her capacity for ministering, caring and spiritual stamina? From the only source available to us as Christians, a life spent in prayer.

In a world that holds so much misery and pain it is good to know that there are people who work tirelessly to ease the burden and bring about some fun and comfort.

KATE'S POEM

Who is this person who cared for me
Who is he that stays beside me?
I think he has got me mixed up with someone else
I'm sure he has 'cause if he knew me he'd be off like a shot
But he seems in no hurry to leave my side. I'm very sure he
made a mistake.
Why does he hang around me when I'm angry and frown
Why does he sit there smiling at me - "go - shoo. Leave me
alone".
I've nothing to give, my body is worn from years of abuse
There is no strength in it - My heart is worn from years of
fear and abuse and pain.
My eyes are dim and dark from years of shame
My hair is worn and torn from pulls and clouts

My ears are blocked from shouts and screams - mental abuse
But my hands, yes my hands they are still in use - they are
hard
But I can still cradle and sooth the sick and dying
Yes, my hands are still OK.
My mind - every one tore at it, what I had, they abused
They shout "you crazy, stupid" and no-one would use me
anymore
But He does not seem to care, it's as if He never heard all I
had to say.
His smile is so, so beautiful I'm sure He thinks I'm someone
else
His eyes are gentle, they shine so bright but it does not hurt
my eyes
He seems to be reaching out to me, he has something in his
hands
A beautiful garment. Clean, pure, it's for me!
I can't - I cry. I've nothing to give - but He still gives it to
me
I turn away - take off my worn-out body - and put it on
I'm drawn to Him - like a magnet. He holds his arms out
I go to him like a child and sink into his open arms.
In my new garment, I'm there to stay, never to leave his side
A King He is, a Princess now I am.
No, this has not been a mistake.
Come walk with me to meet my King and my Friend.

Kate Grey
November 2004

Wenche

I got to know Wenche through my brother's involvement with Dissimilis – a Norwegian organisation giving people with learning disabilities inspiration and hope. They have a special system for teaching music and put on shows which draw huge crowds. The King came to watch one of the shows. There was a standing ovation and the king, bless him, did not sit down for 20 minutes and so, of course, nobody else did either.

Wenche, despite her disability, writes to me in English and this poem comes from her.

Frozen hands

All around are frozen hands
Let's make a chain of people
Holding hands across the world
Joined hands will open borders
And no hand will suffer in frozen isolation

What a wonderful way to describe love for all, leaving no one out.

Growing Closer

When the world around you falls to pieces, God's presence keeps you going. Bad news affects people in two ways. Some people get bitter. That really does not help – it only hurts you more. Others get drawn closer to God. Although the pain is not taken away there is someone to support you who soothes the ache and makes it easier to bear. Prayer support is helpful and comforting. It is strange how that makes a difference – you know when it is no longer there. Time is a great healer and so is the support of friends. There is no need to say anything – just knowing there are people who care is invaluable.

Filling your time is important, but it is not good when you take on too much. It can suppress your feelings and store up trouble for you later on. God thought of everything when he made us. Tears are there for a reason and to shed them gives great relief.

It is my prayer that other people who have lost a child will be given some comfort through reading my book.

Thank you

This book would never have been completed without the endless patience of Jeff Hooper, the person who knows all the secrets of a computer.

I am also very grateful to Virginia Watts who gave me great encouragement when I was flagging and to Frances Nicholaisen and Deborah Bick who went through my manuscript and found numerous faults. With their help all the wrinkles were ironed out.

Bibliography

From Prison to Pulpit, Vic Jacopson, £5.99

Joni - an unforgettable story, Joni Eareckson Tada Zondervan, £9.99

Living through Grief, Harold Bauman, Lion Publishing, £1.50

The Hiding Place, Corrie ten Boom, Hodder and Stoughton, £7.99